New Expanded Edition
Best Selling Classic

HOW to Write Missionary Letters

Practical tips to make your words come alive

Your letters may influence the total missionary enterprise as much as the work you do on the field.

Alvera Mickelsen

MEDIA ASSOCIATES INTERNATIONAL, INC.
Bloomingdale, Illinois, USA

MEDIA ASSOCIATES INTERNATIONAL
Mill Hill, London, UK

First published in 1961 by
Evangelical Literature Overseas now part of Media Associates International.

ISBN 0-9623741-1-3

TO ORDER COPIES OF THIS BOOK CONTACT:

Media Associates International, Inc.
P.O. Box 218
Bloomingdale, IL 60108-0218, USA
TEL: 630-893-1977, FAX: 630-893-1141
MaiLITTWORLD@cs.com
www.littworld.org

Media Associates International
Concorde House, Grenville Place
Mill Hill, London NW7 3SA
England
TEL: (020) 8906 9768, FAX: (020) 8959 3678

USA and UK prices are:

Quantity	US$ Per Copy excluding shipping*	UK£ Per Copy excluding shipping*
Single Copy	$5.95	£4.00
2-5 copies	$5.40	£3.60
6-10 copies	$5.10	£3.40
11-15 copies	$4.75	£3.20
16-25 copies	$4.50	£3.00
26-35 copies	$4.40	£2.90
36-50 copies	$4.20	£2.80
51-75 copies	$4.10	£2.75
76-100 copies	$3.90	£2.60

For quantities over 100 please query for price.

Prices subject to change without notice.

*Note: Prices do not include shipping.

Printed in the United States of America for the publisher,
Media Associates International, Inc.
Bloomingdale, Illinois, USA

PROLOGUE

Letters for the Twenty-first Century

"The times and technology have changed ...but the principles have not."

Your letters to friends and family back home have a profound effect on the cause of world evangelization. That's why we've continued to publish this little book that Alvera Mickelsen first wrote in 1961. And that's why it has remained popular with so many Christian workers. Times and technology have changed, but the basic principles of writing and telling your story have not.

In this edition we've updated a few sections and added several chapters. We've used some new examples of good letters and offered a few check lists.

Writing a good letter is hard work. We won't pretend it isn't. But a good letter is the catalyst for prayer support and for enlarging the vision of others for what God is doing in the world. It is also the means of planting the seed in the hearts of those who will follow you into cross-cultural service tomorrow. The discipline on your part is small compared to the eternal value of letters that are prayerfully and skillfully written. — MAI

Contents

CHAPTER 1

Prayer Letter Potential

"Good letters help the reader to see that missionaries are intelligent..."

Everyone likes to read a good missionary letter. So, why aren't there more *good* letters? Perhaps it's because good writing is difficult; it requires creative thinking and careful planning. This is not easy for most of us.

Yet the potential results of good prayer letters are so tremendous for the future of missionary work that we dare not miss the opportunities we have to share what we are doing.

What Can a Good Letter do for You?

What are some results of good prayer letters?

- Most important, your missionary prayer letters encourage readers to pray for you, for the people among whom you work and the missionary enterprise as a whole.
- Your letters make known the needs and the opportunities of the work in a particular area and, in turn, enlist consecrated dollars and dedicated workers for missionary service.
- Good letters chart the course of missionary work over time. They address current issues, indicate changes in emphasis and trace political trends that are significant to missions.
- Good letters help the reader to see that missionaries are intelligent, alert Christians who have a sense of humor and a wholesome attitude toward life.

Expecting results from your prayer letters means your words will touch the hearts and minds of your readers.

Attract Attention

If a missionary letter is to fulfill its purpose, it must first be read. "Well," you may be saying, "if I take the trouble to write a letter, those who get it will surely take the trouble to read it." Not necessarily!

Consider for a moment a typical scene. Most American homes are besieged by junk mail that begs to be read. Your letter arrives as part of an average day's stack of three to five form letters. Imagine that the person who opens the mail is a woman. She reads what looks interesting, then dumps the rest into a wastebasket.

What happens to your letter? She takes a quick glance. If it catches her attention, she reads it right away. If your letter is good, she absorbs every line of it and reflects on it for the rest of the day, stopping at times to pray for you as she does her work. She puts it aside to share with her husband and children at dinner or family worship. Over the next few days during her private devotions, she prays for specific items you have mentioned in your letter. The family takes it to prayer meeting, sharing your prayer requests with others.

Your prayer letter is part of the ongoing written record of missionary work that will inspire and challenge both present and future generations.

Suppose that your letter looks unappealing at first glance. The opening paragraph is dull. The woman's conscience won't let her dump it in the wastebasket with the rest of the junk mail; instead, she puts it in a desk drawer to be read when she finds time. The letter lies undisturbed until the drawer is cleaned. A quick look at the date reveals that the letter is old, and it is summarily dumped.

The problem is not merely that this letter failed to attract notice; it impressed upon the woman's mind the thought that missionary work is dull and insignificant. That hastily written letter may have saved a few minutes worth of work but may have lost several years' worth of support for missions.

What can you do to make sure that your letters will be read from beginning to end? You must **attract** and **keep the reader's attention** through the appearance and the content of your letter.

Appearance is important because it draws attention to the content. Your letter must pass this acid test when the reader is opening the stack of mail to decide what to discard and what to read; it must attract attention. Form letters are easily identified, even with an airmail or a first class stamp. If the reader is a personal friend, your name alone will attract attention. Most missionary letters, though, are sent to people who know you only slightly. They'll have to compete for recognition with numerous other letters and magazines.

Your letter must not only look but also be interesting.

The situation is perhaps comparable to packaging at a grocery store. Suppose you go to the grocery store to buy a can of peaches and discover, side by side on the shelf, two different brands at the same price. One has a colorful wrapper with a picture of luscious golden peaches on it; the other has a black and white wrapper with only the word "peaches" on it. You would, under normal circumstances, buy the more attractive can. However, if when you ate the peaches you found them tasteless, you would never buy that brand again, regardless of the packaging. You demand quality as well as appearance.

So it is with your letters. Good design and good copy must walk hand in hand. One is never a substitute for the other. The appearance wins attention while the content keeps the reader's interest.

Use a Computer

Not too many years ago, typewriters (remember those?) limited us both in the writing and in the appearance of our letters. Today we can revise, cut and paste, use the spell check and the grammar check, choose from dozens of type faces and sizes, use bullets and checks and boxes, and take advantage of a lot of features to make our letters attractive. If you've been slow to learn the full features of a word processing program, this might be a good incentive to take a little time and learn them.

One big advantage of the computer is the ability to personalize your letters. You can not only add the names of various friends and supporters, but you can add a note specifically for them.

Write letters that are friendly, informative, honest and specific. Paint word pictures for those who have never been to your country. Give the reader something concrete to pray for in your behalf.

Your mailing list is a valuable asset. Keep it updated. Personal information about individuals and families on your list is also handy to have on file. Personal handwritten notes to those you know better is a nice addition to your regular missionary letters. Your readers will appreciate the extra effort.

Write Person-to-Person

Think first, second and always of your reader. Choose a typical reader — maybe an auto mechanic or a mother with a small child — and write every line with that reader in mind. One missionary pulls out a card with the name and address of one of his readers and writes with that man or woman in mind. You will naturally avoid many of the common weaknesses of missionary letters if you write with a flesh-and-blood person in mind.

You may wish to refer to a particular reader in your letter to emphasize that this reader has a part in your work. One missionary used this technique to interest the reader in literature work:

> Young mothers...after getting your children off to school, stop and take a few minutes to think about the books and other literature-related materials your family members use and take for granted each day.
>
> Think about the pleasure your children receive from story books, picture books, cassette tapes and color books.
>
> Your daily Bible reading provides spiritual strength.
>
> And you relax while reading a few chapters in the latest fiction release.
>
> Have you thought of what it would be like not to have any books, study helps, the Bible or other reading material? Not to be able to read or write? This is the plight in which most Senufo people find themselves. What a challenge confronts us Côte d'Ivoire missionaries to bring this new world of the printed page to Senufo men and women!

Writing with a person in mind will make you realize the importance of clarity. This sentence says almost nothing to the reader: "One time a group of us visited Killam." Add a few details and the picture becomes clear to the reader: "Yesterday two African evangelists and I bicycled 10 miles to Killam, an area where about 300 pygmies live."

"Yesterday Yohan decided to quit work" doesn't tell the reader whether Yohan is male or female, sixteen or sixty, houseboy or evangelist, black or white. How could that reader you are visualizing know these things?

"But," you reply, "I mentioned Yohan in a previous letter." Don't assume that your reader remembers your previous letters. He or she might not have seen the letter that identifies Yohan, or your reader might have read it three months ago. Since that time the reader has read 100,000 words and is enmeshed in problems of work, church and family. Be sure that everything in your letter can be understood without reference to previous letters.

If, when you sit down staring at the computer screen, you find yourself asking, "What do I feel like writing about today?" use the following questions as a guide:

1. "What will interest the reader I have in mind this month?"

2. "What does he or she need to know to gain a penetrating view of my work?"

3. "How can I challenge him or her to pray intelligently and consistently for the work over the next few months?"

As you plan and write your letter, remember that you are not addressing a congregation in church; you are talking to an individual in the privacy of his or her own home. You are writing a letter to a person who is your friend and prayer partner.

CHAPTER 2

Principles to Practice

"The first sentence in your letter is the most important..."

Strong beginnings and memorable endings are two essential principles for good prayer letters. Planning, unity, clarity and integrity are also important.

Plan Ahead

Plan in advance. A good letter requires both spiritual and intellectual preparation. It is rarely achieved by sitting in front of a computer screen or at your typewriter and writing whatever thoughts come to mind.

Plan your letter in prayer. Ask the Lord to guide you to the material that will make missions live for your readers. Keep in mind that your letters have a spiritual ministry to your readers. Your letters should prompt them to seek an ever-deepening walk with Jesus Christ.

- Collect information. Make a file with information about the people and area in which you work. Clip articles from newspapers and magazines published in your area. Jot down notes when national leaders make speeches. Maps, geography books and history books supply facts and figures when you need them. Use your computer to organize information for ready access. Facts and figures can be updated easily.
- Collect interesting letters from other missionaries. These will give you ideas you can adapt for your letters.

- Keep a journal. Scribble your notes in the journal. You may want a file on your computer for journal notes to expedite the process. It takes only a few moments to quickly record bits of description, character sketches or a few significant lines of conversation. Be sure to include how you feel, humorous incidents, successes, prayers you've offered and seen answered. You can never retain such details in your mind.
- Keep a record of the letters you have written. Tracking, charting and grouping of information is something computers can do well. Using a computer enables you to see at a glance what subjects you have covered on which dates. If you wish to keep copies or photocopies of all your letters and have room to do so, go ahead. If you are pinched for storage space, each computer floppy disk will hold many letters and take much less room to store.

Here is an example of a fresh approach that also affirms a ministry by citing a newspaper report. Collecting timely and interesting information made such a letter possible.

Dear Bob + Peggy,

Thanks for your Christmas greeting! It helped make Christmas special for us.

This newspaper clipping shows how important translation is! If it's hard to say "We're friends. We want to help you." what about explaining God's forgiveness, salvation, and how to be born again?? You can't do it in a day. You need to live with the people, learn their language and how they think, and ask God to help you find the right words.

If you'd like to read some good stories about how God helped a translator in Papua New Guinea find the right words, you should read "In Search of the Source" by Neil Anderson and Hyatt Moore. Interested? Let us know.

These are busy days. Ron is in on discussions about principles and programs, finances, personnel, and you name it. Pray for him to have

"**Serenity** to accept the things he can't change,
Courage to change the things he can,
and
Wisdom to know the difference,"

as St. Francis of Assisi prayed--and that Ron will be able to sleep well at night.

Mission to
SOMALIA

Say what? Leaflet shows US need for translators

The Associated Press

MOGADISHU, Somalia — The Marines are here, and they may need a few good men — who can translate.

A leaflet that the US forces are using to win over the Somali people is almost incomprehensible.

"The words are good Somali," translator Mohamed Abdulle Farah said, "but put together in sentences they don't make any sense."

The leaflet has at least three misspelled words, one word that doesn't exist and poor syntax. Copies were distributed Sunday in the village of Beli Dogle, where US Marines made their first foray out of Mogadishu to secure an airfield.

On one side, the leaflet bears a drawing of a black US soldier and a

Begin at the Beginning

The first sentence in your letter is the most important. It grabs the reader's attention and sets the tone of what is to follow. Work hard on the opening sentence.

You don't need a salutation ("Dear One Who Prays," etc.), but use one if it makes you feel more comfortable.

Avoid easing into your letter with a weak opening, such as "It's been a long time since I've written you, but...." Introduce the main idea at once. Here are some possibilities:

- Pose a question. One missionary who had just been transferred from Zaire to Côte d'Ivoire started this way:

  Question: "How can you make a new missionary out of an old one?"

  Answer: "Send her to a new field."

The letter then explained the problems that she faced in starting over as a "new missionary."

Another letter challenged the reader by asking, "What's the sense of praying about a grammar book?" It then surveyed how a grammar book would contribute to the literature program as well as the total missionary enterprise.

The opening question used in this letter arouses the reader's curiosity:

> How many souls can you buy for two cows? This silly question was very important to a young African Christian not long ago.
>
> The chief of a village 25 miles from the mission station sent word saying he would like an evangelist to come to live in his village. Buba answered the call saying, "I will go." However, Buba had just planted a large farm with cotton and bought two cows with money he had been saving for years.
>
> Months went by. Even though Buba promised to go soon he didn't. He could not bear to leave the best cotton farm and the two fattest cows in the area.
>
> One morning he went to feed his cows and found them both dead! Then and there he told his wife, "God has spoken. Tomorrow we go to preach. Get our things ready." They went the next day.

Four weeks later he came back and reported 15 people had already received Christ. A few months went by, and there were 28. Then they were building a church for the 120 who gathered every Sunday!

- Begin with an anecdote or story. This opening grips the reader's attention with its graphic portrayal of a conversion: "*Herroro was drunk, not dead drunk, but in the same kind of stupor he had been in for months or possibly years. Now his heavy blurred voice was saying words which protested against all that he was: 'I want to accept Jesus Christ as my Savior.'*"
- Begin with a startling statement. "*Today I saw the 'tomb' of Mary, the mother of Jesus — right here in Pakistan,*" wrote one missionary. The missionary then recounted the teachings of Islam regarding Mary and Jesus.
- Begin with a statement that summarizes the subject of your letter, such as, "*Islam is awakening the Christian church in Europe because of its swift growth.*"
- Begin with a reference to the reader. One missionary began, "*Are you praying extra hard for us this term? It seems so! How else can we explain our deep joy and rich blessings since our return to Argentina? Take, for example, the joy of hearing two young fellows ask, 'Isn't there a village we can evangelize all by ourselves?'*"

Here's a good opening for a letter which had an enclosure:

No, no, don't lay that tract down, you must read it or the rest of this letter won't make sense.

Like it? Here's how an ELWA listener in Tanzania responded. "Your tract sank deep into my heart. In fact, it led me to Jesus Christ as my Savior."

Know why he liked it and came to the Lord? He was familiar with the country fable upon which it was based, and the expressions were African. It was written for him!"

Starting with a Bible verse is rarely effective. Since the reader will not know its relevance until he finishes the letter, he is apt to skip the verse and start to read below it. Put the Bible verse in the body of the letter and within context.

There are countless ways to begin a letter, but whatever one you choose, be sure it reflects the rest of the letter's subject and mood.

Master the Memorable Ending

Prompt the reader to pray for you and your work with a trenchant ending. A 1-2-3 list of prayer and praise items at the end of the letter is often very helpful to the reader, providing you have laid the groundwork in the body of the letter. On the other hand, in many good letters, the subjects for prayer have already been impressed upon the reader and the 1-2-3 list seems superfluous.

When the letter is finished, just stop. Some letters give the impression that the writer is groping for a graceful close. As a result, the letter just "runs down."

Do your readers know for sure **who** you are and **where** you are when they set your letter aside to pray? Always sign both your first and last names. The reader may know three men named "Bill" in Zaire. Don't keep him or her guessing.

Also, put your full address in every letter. You may also help your readers find their bearings by drawing a thumbnail sketch of your country (or continent) and marking an X on your spot. The average reader probably does not know where Burkina Faso, Sri Lanka or Suriname are located.

Strive for Unity

Decide the thrust of your letter before you begin to write. A letter that focuses on one idea or incident is more forceful. A lack of unity is the most common fault of missionary letters.

There are three principle ways of attaining unity: unity through subject; unity through incident; unity through theme.

To attain unity through subject, isolate a subject and treat it thoroughly. Most readers will welcome the informative, meaty letter that results from limiting yourself to one subject.

Don't be afraid of subjects that are difficult or deep. More letters err by being too shallow than by being too deep. There is a maxim that most writers underestimate the intelligence and overestimate the facts at the disposal of the reader on any particular subject. This is especially true of missionaries. Most readers will grasp the point you are trying to make in your letter if you supply them with all the facts they need.

What kind of subjects should you treat? These are a few possibilities that you can adapt to almost any field:

- the religious beliefs of the people among whom you work
- the problems of raising a family in a foreign culture
- the headaches and the heartaches that accompany each stage of planting a local church in a foreign culture
- the obstacles faced by converts in your area
- the contribution your specialized work (agriculture, church planting, education, literature, medicine, radio, etc.) makes to the growth of the church
- the rise of nationalism and its effect on the church
- a new opportunity for expanded witness
- a story of a man or woman who describes his or her growth in the Lord

The list could go on and on.

To attain unity through incident, report a single event in your letter. For example, tell the story of how a church was started, how a family was brought to Christ or how a local Christian witnessed for Christ through sorrow.

The following example illustrates the potency of the single-story letter:

> Just a few short years ago a pastor from the plains of Taiwan wearily toiled up the steep slope of one of the rugged mountains which forms the backbone of this verdant island. Behind him were several hours of trail with almost no respite from the sun. Ahead was a small tribal village perched precariously on a shoulder of the mountain, a village that never had heard the gospel. What would be their response to this strange but wonderful message?

Several hours later his heart was rejoicing over the many who had heard and especially for the one who had believed in Christ. But there was only ONE. Was it worth the long trip? That pastor for some unknown reason never returned, but as the days passed, the Holy Spirit was at work watering the seed.

That one became two, and the two became more as they talked of this new religion. Gradually almost the entire village in a very simple way put their trust in Jesus as they met to recall the pastor's words. From somewhere came an old Japanese Bible and a songbook, and they grew in the Lord.

Word spread down the mountain to another village in the valley like the flying sparks of a fire touching their hearts. It wasn't long until all but a handful in that village also had believed. After a long day's work in their little mountainside fields they would meet to sing with such volume and simple beauty that it must have made the courts of heaven ring.

Recently there have been temptations for these folk who are poor in material things. Not long ago some religious leaders said, "We will give you clothes and milk powder, and you can smoke and drink, if you will join us and form a group." It was a sore temptation, but they stood firm and resisted. Then they asked Stan and me to come and explain more fully the Scriptures.

So we, armed with a shovel and pick to get over the rugged logging road, and with visuals and flannelgraph for the folk to see, bounced in as far as the car could possibly go. Then we walked across a long, rickety suspension bridge that should have fallen in years ago, and climbed the steep trail toward the village. The folks met us with a royal welcome and carried everything, even our Bibles, for us.

When we arrived at the cluster of mud brick and wooden houses with their straw, slate or hand-made shingle roofs, we were met by a crowd who shook our hands and greeted us with "Peace." We were dumbfounded — when had they learned to shake hands? It isn't a usual custom down on the plains.

They treated us like royalty and gave us the best they had. The house was furnished with a table and four benches. Some old snapshots were hanging on walls papered with old newspapers. Chickens and dogs wandered in and out over the mud floors.

Somewhere the villagers got hold of an old Japanese generator, and they were in the process of putting lights in all the houses. Each house was allowed one 15-watt bulb on a long cord which could be carried from the kitchen to the main room as needed.

It was about 9 o'clock that night when they pounded the iron bar gong, and everyone packed into the little rough-hewn church. They sang the old plaintive mountain tunes with Christian words.

The next morning Stan spent about four hours with a little group answering Bible questions and searching out important Bible teachings. Then as we prepared to go back down the mountain and were shaking hands with everyone again, I thanked the Lord that he had allowed us to see his handiwork in the lives of simple mountain villagers.

To attain unity through theme, choose one dominant idea and develop it through a number of instances. Through the theme of "heartbeat" the following letter of a nurse forged a link between medicine and evangelism.

This morning, like every Saturday morning, after the hospital work was under control, I slipped into the "zala" (delivery) room to examine expectant mothers. The stethoscope amazes them, for they probably can't understand how I can listen and learn about something I can't see.

It took us so very much longer today because I endeavored to ask all my routine questions in Kinyuranda. Another language, you ask. Yes, another language, and when I use the stethoscope and listen for heartbeats of little Zaire-folk-to-be, I realize that I must conquer the tribal language if I ever want to know the heartbeat of these Wanyuranda folk.

At the beginning of the new year, I made a vow that I would conquer one lesson a week for the coming year. This week finds me still on the fourth lesson! Why? The wards have been full with little kiddies these days as an epidemic of measles has swept through the Bible school and Christian village. We haven't lost a life yet, thanks to the doctor's good medicine and God's watchcare over them.

Note how the following letter centers around the "Learners" theme:

> One day in Minneapolis a veteran missionary told us, "During your first term remember you are always walking around with a big letter L on you. That L signifies LEARNER. You will be nothing but a LEARNER through your entire first term." How true those words have been! How often we have reminded each other that we are still only LEARNERS.
>
> We've been LEARNING what it feels like to be a foreigner — to live in a strange land amidst a strange people who speak a strange language and have such strange customs. We wonder why everyone insists on eating supper at 9 p.m. Ridiculous! And only a piece of bread and a cup of coffee for breakfast. And why do they clap their hands at the front gate instead of knocking on the door? Or why does Carlos come and chat endlessly before telling us he wants to borrow the bike? Why doesn't he ever get to the point and be frank like the Americans? And why are folks so easily offended when we say we haven't time to stay? When will we LEARN that we MUST stay and visit an hour, or it's better not to go at all?
>
> The Latins are polite people and we must LEARN to be the same — to always greet the meatman, the storekeeper, the postman and ask how the family is before making our purchase. We must adjust to these people and their ways because this is their country. We are the foreigners.

Unity should not be confused with uniformity; thus, aim for variety in the type of letters you write. While you should put to good use your talent for a certain type of letter, you will give a more interesting and complete picture of your work if you vary the handling of your letters from time to time.

Don't depend on feeling or intuition for this. Prepare a chart of the type of letters you have written for the past several months or years. Then resolve to fill in the gaps by writing about topics which you have consistently omitted.

Did something funny, unusual, encouraging, sad, dramatic or a spiritual breakthrough happen today? Don't forget to add it to your computer journal for future reference. You may forget it next week, but your computer entry has stored those ideas for future retrieval.

Be Dramatic

Drama is produced when your letter strikes a balance between showing and telling the reader what happened. This letter shows a linguistic team in action, then offers an explanation:

If you were to eavesdrop at our door these days, you might hear something like this:

"Mo fungi nying" (cool off your insides)...That would be Sagbana telling our informant not to get excited and not to talk so fast while we are trying to write down his words.

"Have him say that again with the negative word after it. I want to see if that verb has all low tones or if it comes up to a midtone on the end."

"I want to play some of this back on the tape to see if this man's voice is recording clearly and loudly enough."

"Did you hear the down-glide on that tone and how long he made the vowel? I suspect that's just a contraction of their midtone pronoun and the low-tone indicator which tells you the verb is in the future."

This is our "team" at work getting material to compare all the important language dialects on our field. We have 23 pages of words and sentences which cover main grammatical constructions as well as all the possible tone patterns on nouns and verbs in our dialect. We are hard at work to get these same words and sentences from each of the other dialects to make comparisons. This, in turn, will help us know which dialects can be reached with the same translation of the Scriptures, with the same literacy materials, by a missionary speaking another dialect.

This is how the laborious process works: Robert Wallace goes out and brings back an informant to the station. There he records all the material on tape, and at the same time Sharon Wallace and I write it down on paper. Sharon's sharp ears pick up difficult tone variations and changes. Often we use three languages in the process (four, counting the comments among ourselves in English). Robert gives a word in French to Sagbana; Sagbana says it in the Dyoula (jewel-ah) trade language to the informant, who in turn repeats it in his own dialect. Then we must catalog and analyze what we have compiled.

Three years ago today I flew from New York to this mission field in

Côte d'Ivoire. How I praise the Lord for His continual faithfulness and for every experience He has brought into my life! Thank you, too, for your gifts and prayers which have made it possible for me to serve the Lord here.

Dramatic stories are not always available. But often missionaries fail to see the essential drama around them.

One missionary wrote a thrilling account of a mule trip in the Andes Mountains. The missionary who accompanied him on the trip later said, "I got more excited when I read Jerry's account of the trip than I did on the trip itself!" The writer did not exaggerate or dress up the facts; he simply sensed what was truly dramatic about what seemed prosaic at the time.

Develop a keen sense of **sight, sense, sound, taste** and **touch** when you write. Appeal to the senses. This allows the reader to enter more fully into the experience.

Use dialogue whenever possible. Few things spark up a letter (or any written material) as well as several lines of good dialogue. Incidentally, good dialogue is a condensed version of what people actually say and the way they say it.

Note how dialogue improves this letter:

"And what can I do?" That question! At times it has caused my ire to rise, and other times I have felt defeated by it. So often it is used as an answer, and in many ways it describes the outlook of the people. For instance: In the hospital the child won't take the medicine so the parents say, *"The child says, 'No,' so what can we do?"*

Parents complain about a naughty child, *"He won't listen to me. What can I do?"* If it were only a matter of a few days' teaching them to have a different outlook, it would be a small thing. But this idea of being unable to do anything carries over into every phase of life.

In the hospital we had a six-year-old child severely burned on the back; therefore, we kept him lying on his stomach. Oh, how that child cried to lie on his back! Hearing his cries the parents put him on his back. I asked them, "Why have you done this?"

"He cried to lie on his back, and what could we do?" they answered.

Day by day we had to watch carefully that the parents didn't turn him on his back.

It was time to remove the dressings and allow the burns to heal using the heat cradle. The mother kept saying, "Put dressings on the burns, put dressings on the burns." We showed her how much better the child was getting, explaining how this was the best treatment. She wouldn't have it. Finally the father came to me saying, "How much is our bill? We are going home." Surprised I asked, "Why are you going home?" "The mother can't stand to see the burns not dressed. She says to go home. And what can I do?" he said.

"You're the head of the house," I replied. "You can say, 'Stay here,' and they'll stay. If you take that child home, he'll die. If he dies it will be your fault. What kind of love is this?"

After trying my best to persuade them to stay, they insisted on signing the child out of the hospital. Later he died. The parents brought me the news, saying, "It was his fate; that's why he died. And what could we do?"

Many carry this same question over into the spiritual realm. How many, many times after explaining the way of salvation so clearly have I been faced with the question, "It's all in God's hands. What can we do?"

PRAY for parents who fail to see their responsibilities. And PRAY for me for perseverance to continue to do what is necessary.

Don't be afraid to condense five minutes of actual talk into five lines. Don't write sermons, not even short ones. Your readers hear lots of sermons. They read devotional books. You have something which you can give them — news of the Lord's work in your particular area.

At Christmas, Easter and Thanksgiving many missionaries replace their regular letter with a short seasonal meditation or poem. It may seem like the easy way out, but resist the temptation. Your sermons are less likely to be read at Christmas than at any other time. Most people barely have time to open Christmas cards and observe the name on the bottom, much less to read "sermonettes"; but they will read a letter that with a few deft strokes depicts how people in another part of the world observe

Christmas. By the way, if you do decide to use someone else's poem or other written text at any time, do observe copyright laws. Write to ask permission from the author or publisher before using any published material.

Be Clear

Don't worry about being clever or developing a literary style. Do worry about being clear and making sure the reader easily and fully understands what you are saying. Above all, don't use pious phraseology in the effort to "sound like a missionary." Use the kind of language which comes naturally to you.

Translate all terminology which may not be understood by all your readers. In many countries, distance is measured in kilometers instead of miles. Your reader may not know how far 80 kilometers is; translate it into 50 miles. Likewise, the values of foreign currencies — francs, pesos, rupees, shillings — are second nature to you; they are not to your reader. Many other terms — such as mela, catechumen or gendarme — that constantly appear in missionary letters require an explanation or a substitution.

Identify people and places. "Ben Olson, our field director," or "Olufemi Oni, our national pastor," facilitates understanding. "Lagos, the capital of Nigeria," cues in the reader to geography. Lest you think the reader ought to know such things, ask yourself how many capital cities you know on a continent other than the one in which you work.

Be specific. Avoid vague statements, such as "Pray for a very real need we face at present," or "I'm much stronger after my long illness." Such euphemisms are maddening to the reader. They make him feel left out, as though you were writing to someone else who knows the answers to "what need?" and "what illness?" Either say more or don't say anything at all.

Aim for simple, uncluttered sentences. The subject-predicate order is the easiest to read and to understand. Beware of sentences that only make sense when you reach the end.

A sentence that requires unnecessary backtracking is awkward: "Because of the disillusionment and sense of bewilderment which followed the war, the Japanese people, for a period, listened eagerly to the gospel." This sentence is much easier to comprehend when it is shortened and every part of it made to move forward: "The Japanese people were disillusioned and bewildered after the war. During this post-war period, they listened eagerly to the gospel."

Any sentence that exceeds 30 words demands scrutiny; it might benefit from being divided in two. Most sentences in missionary letters are too long and contain too many ideas. A single sentence should not constitute a whole long paragraph. While a succession of short (10 to 12 word) sentences makes letters choppy, few err in that direction.

Short paragraphs are usually easier to read than long paragraphs. They also make a letter look more interesting.

Rambling accounts of day-to-day activities are better suited to a diary than to a missionary letter. An appalling number of letters seem composed primarily of "last week we had a meeting in village A with 20 people there; then we drove home and got a night's sleep, and the next day we visited the out schools around village B, and that night we had a meeting in village C..." and on and on and on. An annual summary of the number of meetings held, or patients treated or villages visited may be in order if these facts enlighten and are significant.

Check your letter for grammatical correctness. (If you are unsure of the rules of grammar, ask someone to help you.)

Most word processing programs have grammatical helps as well as spelling and thesaurus features. Use them! Use a dictionary regularly. Misspelled words leap from the page and stay longer in the minds of some readers than the content of the letter. Often these glaring errors are simply the result of careless keystrokes; and often you are too hurried or too close to the letter to notice them. Don't depend completely on the computer's spell check. Computers can't catch mistakes such as wrong word choices or singular-plural errors. Furthermore, such errors make you look illiterate to sharp high school and college students who should be challenged for missionary work. Subconsciously they may think that missionary work is for the not-so-bright people.

Revise and rewrite your letter at least once. Professional writers habitually rewrite two or more times. After your first draft is finished, lay it aside for a day. When you open the letter file again, imagine that you are a mechanic in a small town or a young suburban mother and read it through their eyes. You'll see the sentences which are not clear, which give a wrong impression or supply irrelevant material.

Maintain Integrity

Integrity means wholeness and honesty. Assume for our purposes that your letters are the only contact the readers have with missions. Are they getting a fair, comprehensive, realistic picture of missionary work — the plans, the disappointments, the victories and the future possibilities?

Keep the readers in touch with your family and its progress, but don't let the family dominate your letters. Write about how animism, Buddhism, communism, fatalism, Islam or other beliefs threaten or impede missionary work in your area. Don't make all your letters historical, religious or sociological treatises.

Be generous with stories about the people among whom you work. Let readers see them as people with the same feelings and sorrows and joys that they experience. Only then are your readers truly compelled to pray for them.

The poignant plea for prayer in the following excerpt about money is effective largely because of the insight it gives into individual lives:

> One of the biggest problems which a missionary faces on the field is MONEY. Please don't misunderstand me in thinking that I mean the lack of it, or that this is a plea for money. It is not, because the Lord provides according to our needs. The real problems have to do with handling funds entrusted to us. Let me give some examples.
>
> What would you do?
>
> - If two out of three daughters eligible for girls' camp could not attend because the parents did not have sufficient money to pay the travel expenses of them all;
> - If a talented young man desiring to be a medical doctor in a Christian hospital lacked funds for his education partly because his father was in the Lord's work;
> - If your workers suffered a sudden loss of money and possessions because they were caught in mob rioting while traveling to your station;

- If, because in their eyes you are rich, you face constant begging from people you want to have as friends.

Please pray that I may have wisdom from the Lord in dealing with money problems, that I may have a sympathetic understanding of the real needs, and that I may be able to deal with each individual with kindness and love.

Treat people of other cultures with respect and sympathy in your letters. One missionary said he never wrote anything in his letters that he wouldn't be willing to have anyone from his adopted country read. Whenever possible it is important that your letters help the reader to look at problems from your adopted cultural vantage-point.

Missionaries **can** exert influence on the perceptions of the public by exercising responsible leadership. Many members of the public think that the American cultural brand of Christianity is the fountainhead of wisdom and the dispenser of all that is good. You can cater to the readers' petty provincialisms, or you can bring them up-to-date on current events in the church at large.

Make use of humor when possible. One of the basic rules of psychology is that people turn away from what is unpleasant. Humor not only lightens but balances the load your letter is carrying. Missionary work is difficult, but it is not grim. Humor adds interest with a chuckle and makes entertaining reading. Recounting humorous experiences can help you gain perspective and keep a healthy attitude.

Funny, sympathetic stories about the people with whom you work are fine if they don't belittle. Even better are stories that make **you** the butt of the joke. Your life is full of funny things — language errors, misunderstandings about the culture in which you live, and so forth. When readers see that you are able to laugh at **yourself,** they'll like you better. The deeper their affection for you, the more natural it becomes for them to pray for you.

Be honest about your feelings and reactions in your letters. This missionary's candor is refreshing: "Returning home we were itchily aware that we were taking something from the village with us. A couple of us were covered from head to foot with flea bites before we finally got rid of the pests. But the blessings of rich fellowship and seeing what the Lord had done were worth all the misery of scratching during the following days!"

Don't paint glowing portraits of a work that doesn't really glow. Highlight the victories whenever you can, but don't hesitate to reveal the discouragements, the hard problems and the defeats. Give an accurate, well-balanced picture of your work.

Here are questions to ask yourself as you write and rewrite your letter:

1. Have I committed this letter to the Lord in prayer?
2. Does my beginning sentence and paragraph grab the reader's attention?
3. Did I write the way I talk? Does my letter sound like me?
4. Did I share what I really wanted to say?
5. Is my letter interesting and informative as well as truthful? Can I make the facts of my story more interesting by writing poignantly, dramatically, humorously or in another style?
6. Will people, places and events mentioned be clear to my readers?
7. Is my letter concise? Do I need to cut unimportant or unnecessary details?
8. Is the ending to my letter memorable? Will it call my reader to action?
9. Did I check grammar, punctuation and spelling?
10. Is my full name and mailing address on my letter?

The answer to all these questions should be yes. If any answer is no, you'll know what to work on.

CHAPTER 3

Picture Your Letter on Paper

"Vary the form of your letter..."

You can often greatly improve the appearance of your letter without additional expense or undue labor. After you've written or typed the first draft, format a rough layout. Take another look at your letter, and rewrite it carefully. Set it up to leave room for illustrations, headings and so forth. Then lay it aside for a day or two. Often this space — this distance — will enable you to approach your letter afresh and see what needs changing, where to cut, what to add or how to make the stories in your letter come alive for your reader. Keep in mind the following pointers:

Keep It Simple

The appearance of the letter should enhance rather than detract from its content. If an intricate format or unusual design makes your letter hard to read, skip it. Restrict handwritten copy to signatures and personal notes added to finished letters.

Don't crowd your letter. Plan to leave a space between paragraphs and to have generous margins on all four sides. An absolute minimum for margins is one inch. Always be sure the typeface is reader friendly. Some typefaces impede the reader. For example, don't write the whole letter in italics, script or a very small typeface.

Decide the length of your letter in advance. One-page letters are usually read and therefore more effective.

If your draft letter spills onto the second page, don't worry. Remember, this is your first draft. Put down your thoughts first, then revise, polish and edit later. Cutting excess lines during rewrite strengthens your letter. During rewrite sessions you will have an opportunity to choose, change and prune words to have the best flow of thought in your letter. And, while we're talking about rewriting, please use double spacing for your first draft. This makes it easier to add to and correct your copy.

Most missionaries who write frequently cover only one side of a single page. Some subjects, however, cannot be handled adequately on a single page. If you are sure the subject merits more than one page, write the second page with a clear conscience.

Use the Resources at Hand

The computer offers lots of possibilities to make your letter inviting to read. However, it's just as easy to misuse these features and end up with a confusing eyesore. Don't use type faces less than 11 points, especially if many of your readers are getting into their fifties or more. Use a little appropriate clip art here and there if you have it to break up the long gray pages of type. But don't overdo it.

If you use colored paper be sure it's a very light shade and make sure the type face is 12 point. Otherwise you reduce the legibility. You can't guarantee readership, so make it as easy to read as possible.

THE FIRST DELIVERY IS HISTORY: Native women have been coming to the dispensary for pre-natal care, and one reported as usual that morning. Then about noon the Woodcutter called Peg saying that a woman was dying out in the brush.

Peg went out to find the woman sitting in the weeds about 20 yards behind the dispensary, holding her new-born baby.

She had followed the native custom and delivered her baby in the brush even though she had been to the dispensary so many times. When she and the baby were cared for, the mother took her precious prize, wearing a new shirt and wrapped in a soft blanket and walked home, possibly several miles.

THIS, TOO, IS MISSIONARY LABOR: We kept track of our guests for one month and were interested to find that we and another missionary couple entertained 92 overnight guests and served 208 guest meals. Wouldn't you all like to drop in? No, we are not running a hotel, but members of our own mission family and others find it necessary to come as they enter eastern Zaire, leave on furlough via Bukavu or come because of business. Our thatched guest house is an attempt to give the visitors a place to stay while we try to carry on the regular work with as little interruption as possible.

If you have some drawing skill, a few figures can add a personal touch to your letter. You can buy CD's with hundreds of pieces of clip art, although it's sometimes hard to find just the right one that fits.

Start your own file, too, of clippings from national newspapers and magazines. Trace simple outlines from the pictures and use them in your letters to portray what life is like in the country where you serve. (You will not violate any copyright laws in so doing.)

If the drawings you find do not exactly fit, you may alter them slightly to suit your purposes. One missionary drew caricatures of himself by adding a pair of glasses and a shock of unruly hair to the pictures he traced from various sources.

Put photographs in your letters. You'll be amazed at the impact of a letter with photographs. Carefully chosen photographs can help inform your readers and provide emotive value to your letters. Readers will be drawn to read your letter because of a well-placed photo. Readers at home will appreciate photographs because they have never been to your country. So keep your camera handy. You never know when you might find a good subject or activity to snap. Take action shots. Photograph people at work.

Show examples of life in your adopted culture through photography. Steer clear of the photograph in which a group of people stare into the camera. Sharp, dramatic shots that capture someone doing something are welcome.

Be sure the photo is in focus and has good contrast. Most photos lose some detail in the printing process. A fuzzy, gray photograph will look even worse when it is reproduced.

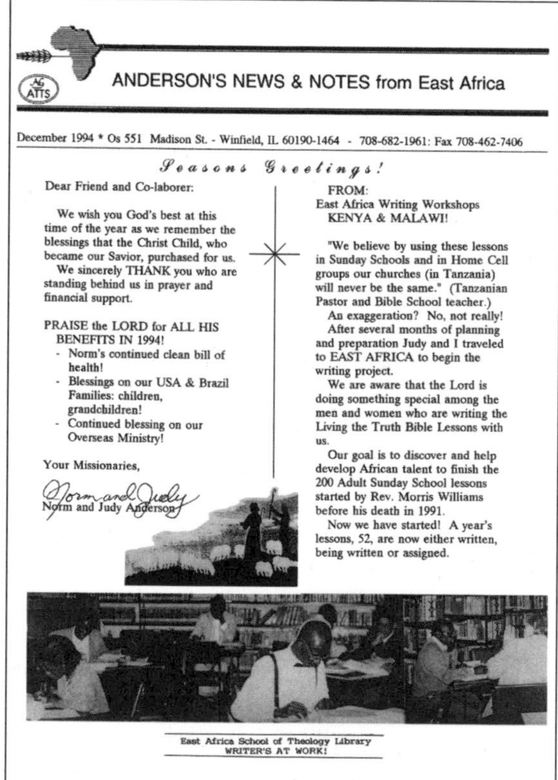

ANDERSON'S NEWS & NOTES from East Africa

December 1994 * Os 551 Madison St. - Winfield, IL 60190-1464 - 708-682-1961: Fax 708-462-7406

Seasons Greetings!

Dear Friend and Co-laborer:

We wish you God's best at this time of the year as we remember the blessings that the Christ Child, who became our Savior, purchased for us.

We sincerely THANK you who are standing behind us in prayer and financial support.

PRAISE the LORD for ALL HIS BENEFITS IN 1994!

- Norm's continued clean bill of health!
- Blessings on our USA & Brazil Families: children, grandchildren!
- Continued blessing on our Overseas Ministry!

Your Missionaries,

Norm and Judy Anderson

FROM:
East Africa Writing Workshops
KENYA & MALAWI!

"We believe by using these lessons in Sunday Schools and in Home Cell groups our churches (in Tanzania) will never be the same." (Tanzanian Pastor and Bible School teacher.)

An exaggeration? No, not really!

After several months of planning and preparation Judy and I traveled to EAST AFRICA to begin the writing project.

We are aware that the Lord is doing something special among the men and women who are writing the Living the Truth Bible Lessons with us.

Our goal is to discover and help develop African talent to finish the 200 Adult Sunday School lessons started by Rev. Morris Williams before his death in 1991.

Now we have started! A year's lessons, 52, are now either written, being written or assigned.

East Africa School of Theology Library
WRITER'S AT WORK!

Add Variety

Vary the form of your letter. Arrange paragraphs in new patterns or cast headings in bold-face type. The unusual approach to form in the following letter invites the reader's participation:

QUIZ YOURSELF

We sometimes get questionnaires from people who are interested in our work, so we thought we would reverse things and let you quiz yourself about missions in Francophone Africa. Here we go:

1. CHECK WHICH OF THE FOLLOWING IS A PART OF A MISSIONARY'S WORK

- ☐ Building a house.
- ☐ Learning the language.
- ☐ Transporting sick people to dispensaries or hospitals.
- ☐ Translating Scriptures and other literature.
- ☐ Answering letters.
- ☐ Keeping house.
- ☐ Killing snakes, scorpions, spiders, etc.

2. TRUE-FALSE

______ Missionaries are "super-human" and can do no wrong.

______ Dispensing medication to the sick and prayer are equally vital in the missionary's daily life.

______ Missionaries are never discouraged.

______ A letter from YOU could bring encouragement to a missionary.

______ Children of missionaries in Francophone Africa must attend school far from their parents eight months of each year for the sake of their health.

3. MULTIPLE CHOICE

African people most need: ☐ clothing ☐ food ☐ Christ

African languages are: ☐ easily learned ☐ impossible to learn
☐ learnable but very difficult

The tribes in northern Côte d'Ivoire have heard the Gospel story:
☐ often ☐ never ☐ seldom

Who should pray for spreading the Word?
☐ the pastor ☐ the head deacon ☐ yourself ☐ every Christian

4. STATE IN 25 WORDS (OR MORE):

"My part in telling the gospel in Francophone Africa is ________

____

____

If you checked all of Part 1, you're so right! This is only a partial list.

I think the True-False of Part 2 are quite obvious, but perhaps we need to be reminded of these things.

Part 3 is there to remind you of our Africans who need Christ. Most of them have never heard of Him and their language is very difficult, but learnable.

You ask the Lord to check your answer to Part 4.

I hope you made a good score. Perhaps you can use the quiz this month as an outline as you pray for us and the Lord's work in the Côte d'Ivoire.

Indenting lines or paragraphs can add visual interest to your letter. Another way is to indent important paragraphs on both the right and the left sides.

Indentation and the poetic form of the following letter make the words leap out at the reader:

Dear Friends:

It makes a difference where you are. Today sub-zero weather
in these northern states brings out:
Heavier clothing, warm gloves and boots.

The scraping sound of snow shovels,
The smell of applied remedies for colds and coughs,
The hurry to the service station for anti-freeze for your car,
because it's mid-winter in this part of their country.

But, if you were in Quepe, Chile, today, you'd forget coats and colds and you'd
Follow the young people to morning Bible classes this week of camp,
Wipe the perspiration away after your game of volleyball,
Enjoy a refreshing swim in the river before supper,
Sit around the campfire tonight and hear Gospel tunes and
Pray in English as the Gospel is preached in Spanish, now that it's mid-summer in Chile.

It made a difference being in the U.S. this year because it:
United me with loved ones after six years' absence,
Opened doors of witness in many parts of the country,
Provided physical rest and change (and added pounds!).
Brought heaps of memories to treasure and share when back in Chile for the next six years. (Unless He comes sooner.)

Your prayers will make a difference as you ask for:
Chilean Customs officers not to demand exorbitant duty on baggage,
A rapid adjustment made as I resume third-term duties in Chile,
A spiritual awakening at the Youth Convention Easter Week,
Our 25 Christian grammar schools and teachers as school year begins in March,
Those doing follow-ups with summer campaign converts,
The Bible Institute in Temuco and young people training there,
Permits to be granted Mr. Strong to continue preaching to the military.

What a difference our Lord Jesus makes in all of life! Going back to Chile is:
Not a duty, to be faced unflinchingly. It's a privilege!
Nor a way of wiping out the debt I owe Him for dying for me. I never could repay that debt.
Not the result of pity for Chileans. They neither want nor need it.
I go in love because He asks me to go and
Because He asks, I cannot stay.

Thank you for your gifts, letters, cards, prayers and every kindness.

Yours in Him Whose love never fades,

The following letter incorporates different typefaces, boxes, photos, and plenty of white space. But again, don't overdo the use of various type faces.

African Byh Lines

Jim & Kristi Byh
Missionaries to
Benin, West Africa

Dear Partners in the Great Commission,

Greetings in the wonderful name of our Savior!

"Unless the Lord builds the house, its builders labor in vain.
Unless the Lord watches over the city, the watchmen stand guard in vain."

THE LORD IS BUILDING HIS CHURCH IN BENIN

In two key northern Muslim-dominated cities, Malanville and Kandi, the Church of Jesus Christ has been planted. In the city of Malanville, which borders the desert country of Niger, there was no evangelical church. Today, by the grace of God, the light of Jesus is shining in this unreached city. Please pray that the Lord would watch over these brand new churches as they grow and develop.

New church roof completed

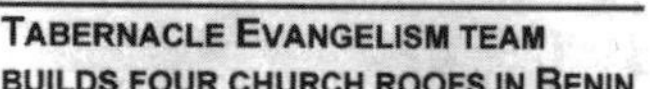

TABERNACLE EVANGELISM TEAM BUILDS FOUR CHURCH ROOFS IN BENIN

A building team from Washington, Illinois, led by Don Bowman, put up four church roofs in strategic locations in Benin. Tabernacle Evangelism is a partnership effort to put roofs in place, thus allowing a new local church to meet together for worship. The local church will then complete the foundation and walls of the building. It was a blessing to see the commitment of the building team and the joy on the faces of African believers who sang praises to God upon completion of the roof of their new church.

Team members taking "five."

THREE NEW CHURCHES ARE BEING PLANNED IN UNREACHED AREAS OF BENIN

Consider a unique format or logo that will immediately identify you and add local color to your letter. One missionary from Argentina draws an outline of mountains with a llama in the foreground on all her letters. Logos can be drawn using a graphics program or drawing program. Once a logo is created on the computer, it can be saved and used to make ordinary paper look like personalized stationery or letterhead.

Shown here are three logos and an excellent example of a personalized letterhead.

Bangkok Bulletin
News from David and Ulla Fewster

PETTINGER HAPPENINGS
in
LESOTHO
"FROM OUR HUT TO YOURS"

Eagles Group: The Bible and Drug Addiction

Besides our own literature projects, Eagles Group also helps other Christian organizations with their literature needs. One of these is the *Bible Society of Egypt*. A recent pamphlet completed for the BSE is entitled "What the Bible Says to Drug Addicts." It tells the story in words and pictures of a young man who fell into the snare of drug abuse, then heard the voice of Jesus and found new life. *Pray for the people reading the 100,000 pamphlets now being distributed throughout the country.*

Other News

- **Nancy and the kids head back to the American International School** this month. Nancy will again teach 2nd grade. Stephanie is now in 3rd, and Christopher is entering Junior High!
- **Two articles Randy wrote on visual communication** have appeared in issues of *David C. Cook Foundation's* publishing journal *Interlit*, based on a lecture he gave at a publishing conference in 1992 sponsored by *Media Associates International.*
- **Nancy finished her courses** this summer (with all "A's") to renew her Kansas pre-school certification. She will continue taking additional courses toward her Illinois elementary education degree, *which may require another trip to the U.S. next summer.*

A Bulgarian pastor we worked with speaks to the crowd gathered in the Kazanluk town hall.

Slava Na Boga: Living Pictures in Bulgaria!

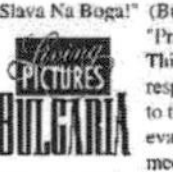

"Slava Na Boga!" (Bulgarian for "Praise the Lord!") This was the response of many to the eight evangelistic meetings in central and eastern Bulgaria. Total attendance was just over 3,000. Three meetings were in former communist halls. One meeting (near the Turkish border) was in the town cinema, which was currently showing the film Dracula! *Many of you told us you were faithfully praying, and we want to thank you!* Plans are underway for future trips.

Thank You
to all who made our summer in America so special!

Journal: On Reliability

We hired her directly from college. I spent countless hours training her on graphic design software, and we hoped she understood the opportunity she was getting. *It was as if Eagles Group sent her to America for study ...except that the teacher came to Egypt instead.*

But as we began to add new staff, Sami Yacoub and I felt the need to make two-year contracts with each staff member. This would guard us from investing training in someone who wouldn't stay.

She was the one person who refused to sign.

I told her, "We can't invest more time in you without a commitment that you use your training to produce Christian books."

We pleaded, "Its not fair to the others if we let you stay without a contract."

She said she liked working with us, but still wanted the freedom to leave at any time. We would not give in. A few weeks later she was gone.

I gained a deeper appreciation for what Paul told Timothy in 2 Timothy 2:2. *"And the things you have heard me say in the presence of many witnesses, entrust to **reliable** men who will also teach others."* The background to this charge came earlier in 1:15, *"You know that everyone in the province of Asia has deserted me."*

I could feel Paul's frustration of wasting time on people who weren't committed for the long haul. He told Timothy, *"Avoid my mistake. Entrust these things to **reliable** people."*

We are now starting to train new people. Pray with us that the Lord will lead us to a reliable staff, building something strong and enduring.

Randy

"Sketches" is the newsletter of Randolph, Nancy, Christopher & Stephanie Capp

Our Egyptian address is: P.O.Box 1101, Heliopolis Bahri 11737, Cairo Egypt. Fax: 202-263-6994.

Mail within the US is forwarded to us by Tim and Karla Felter, 2714 Royal Kings Ct, St. Charles 60174.

We are supported through the D.M.Stearns Missionary Foundation. P.O.Box 1578, North Wales, PA 19454. Tax deductible contributions sent to Stearns for our support must be made out to the D.M. Stearns Missionary Foundation, with a separate note saying it is for the Capps.

Some missionaries adopt a newspaper style for their letters, with columns and headings such as "South Asia Report." As you can see, the format fosters a more brisk handling of the subject:

SOUTH ASIA REPORT

The Len and Diane Stitt Family P.O. Box 7052 Grayslake, IL 60030

Update

Since we sent our summer newsletter, we have continued to make preparations to leave for India. We were supposed to leave in November, but we have had to get an extension of our departure date. The reason for the delay? We have not yet received our visa from the Indian government. Also, we have to finish raising the final portion of our monthly support. Our new departure date is January 31st.

In November, we moved out of the house we were renting and are now living with friends. We will stay with them until we leave the country. We have sold most of our furniture and a lot of our household goods. We will be able to purchase most of the things we need to set up a household after we arrive in India.

We also have begun the task of packing for India. This is a time-consuming process requiring detailed lists of what we are taking and careful packing to protect the contents of each container. Packing will take up a lot of our time, especially during January.

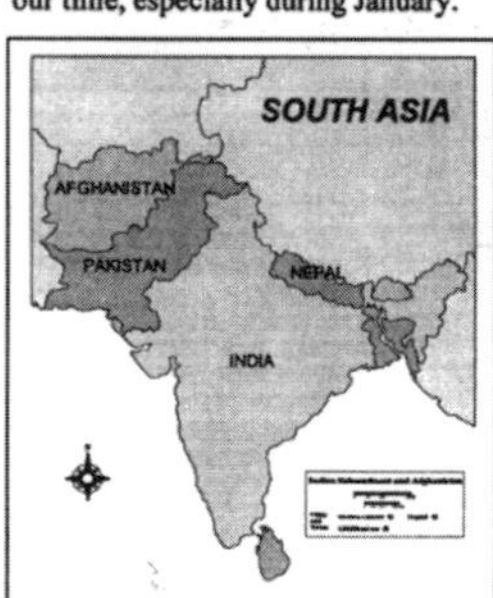

We also are getting ready to visit both of our families during the Christmas holidays. This will likely be our last extended visit with them before we leave. We will be in India for four years, so Christmas this year will be marked by mixed feelings for us.

It seems a bit strange to be telling you about our preparations for leaving the good old USA, but I think that it may be helpful for you to know something of the "practical" side of going overseas. Usually, when we visit in churches we only have time to share the more "spiritual" aspects of our missionary call, but there is a lot of "grunt work" that must be done before we ever step foot on foreign soil.

As we finish up our itineration, we want to say thank you for the many blessings we have received from churches and individuals. We could never have made it this far without you! God bless you!

Items On Islam

During the past few months, there has been significant religious turmoil in South Asia, especially for Christians. A number of Pakistani Christians have been jailed or threatened because of their faith. Unfortunately, this kind of persecution is not unique to South Asia. In a number of countries Christians have been jailed or even put to death. In Iran, for example, several pastors and church leaders have been killed, including the superintendent of the Assemblies of God in Iran and another Assembly of God pastor. The news bulletin *Intercede* had this to say about the situation:

"Even with the current hostilities, Christians say ministry is continuing in Iran and the church is growing. One Iranian pastor, living outside the country, said he believes the latest round of persecution may be the beginning of a 'great revival' in his homeland: 'We believe if the Lord is allowing...the church in Iran to pay such a great sacrifice, He is also going to do a great work in Iran.'"

Please pray for Christians in Iran and South Asia who are facing such enormous difficulties, that God will continue to strengthen their faith and their witness.

Merry Christmas!

May this Christmas season be filled with blessings for you and yours! And may the coming New Year be one of peace and joy.

"Behold, I bring you good tidings of great joy which will be to all people. For there is born to you this day in the city of David a Savior, who is Christ the Lord." Luke 2:10-11

Prayer Requests

As God brings us to your mind, please remember these prayer needs:

- For the remainder of our monthly support to come in before the end of January.
- That our visa will be approved by the Indian government without delays.
- That all of our packing, plane reservations, finding a house to rent in India, and other last minute details will come together for us. There is much to get done!

You may find unique stationery with lots of color or flair for your letters. This missionary family found stationery with illustrations about their adopted country.

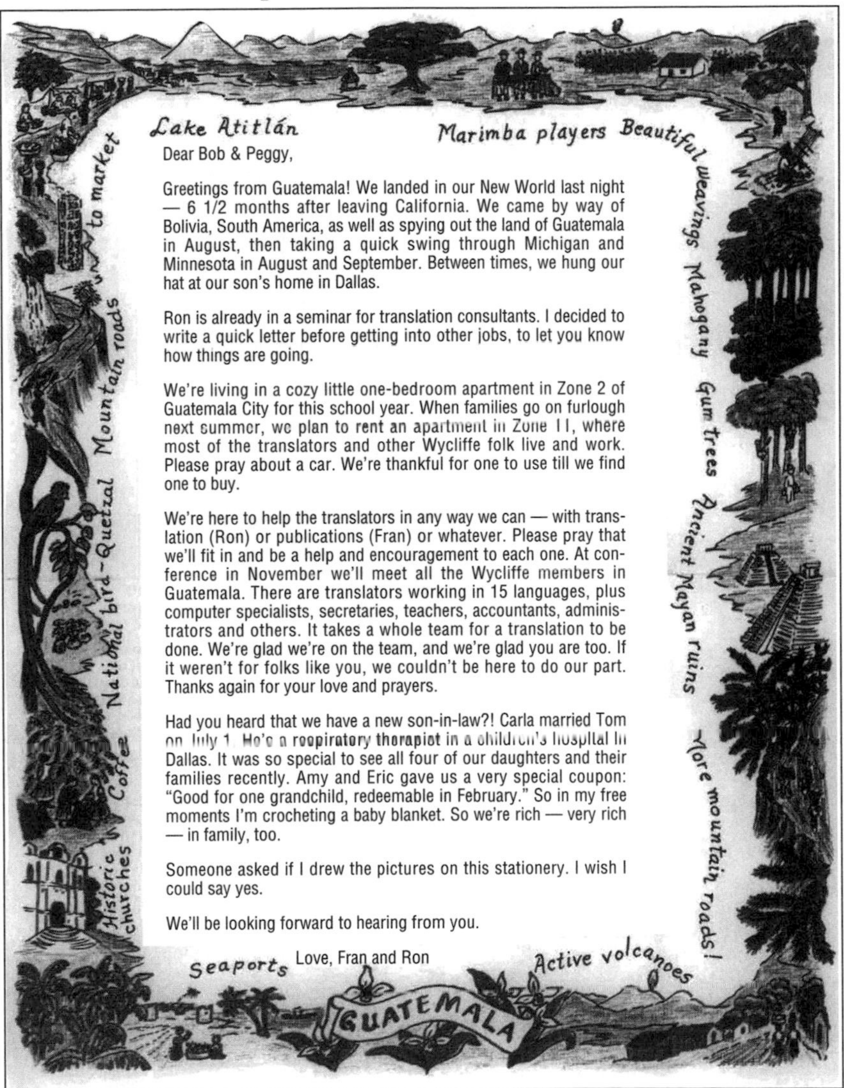

Dear Bob & Peggy,

Greetings from Guatemala! We landed in our New World last night — 6 1/2 months after leaving California. We came by way of Bolivia, South America, as well as spying out the land of Guatemala in August, then taking a quick swing through Michigan and Minnesota in August and September. Between times, we hung our hat at our son's home in Dallas.

Ron is already in a seminar for translation consultants. I decided to write a quick letter before getting into other jobs, to let you know how things are going.

We're living in a cozy little one-bedroom apartment in Zone 2 of Guatemala City for this school year. When families go on furlough next summer, we plan to rent an apartment in Zone 11, where most of the translators and other Wycliffe folk live and work. Please pray about a car. We're thankful for one to use till we find one to buy.

We're here to help the translators in any way we can — with translation (Ron) or publications (Fran) or whatever. Please pray that we'll fit in and be a help and encouragement to each one. At conference in November we'll meet all the Wycliffe members in Guatemala. There are translators working in 15 languages, plus computer specialists, secretaries, teachers, accountants, administrators and others. It takes a whole team for a translation to be done. We're glad we're on the team, and we're glad you are too. If it weren't for folks like you, we couldn't be here to do our part. Thanks again for your love and prayers.

Had you heard that we have a new son-in-law?! Carla married Tom on July 1. He's a respiratory therapist in a children's hospital in Dallas. It was so special to see all four of our daughters and their families recently. Amy and Eric gave us a very special coupon: "Good for one grandchild, redeemable in February." So in my free moments I'm crocheting a baby blanket. So we're rich — very rich — in family, too.

Someone asked if I drew the pictures on this stationery. I wish I could say yes.

We'll be looking forward to hearing from you.

Love, Fran and Ron

As you have seen, varying the format and appearance of your prayer letters can produce attractive eye-catching results. So you will want to look over your prayer letters to consider how you might improve their appearance.

Check your last prayer letter while asking yourself these questions:

1. Did it seem crowded or open?

2. Was it easy or hard to read?

3. Did I alter the form to accentuate the content?

4. Would my prayer partners instantly recognize my letter because of a distinguishing feature?

5. Did I take advantage of available features on my computer?

6. Did I try to format a personal logo or use drawings or photographs and colored paper effectively?

7. Did the nature of my subject justify the length of my letter?

Try using these questions to improve the next prayer letter you write to your readers and prayer partners.

CHAPTER 4

Powerful Furlough Letters

"The impact of a furlough letter can be far reaching..."

Many missionaries are nonplussed as to what to write about, or if they should write at all during furlough. Imagine for a moment a coach who pulls his team off the field during the game. The team will not be able to score any points. The missionary who pulls his letters off the mission field also stands to lose. The answer is plain: If you want your prayer and financial support to continue, you must write regularly.

You can write a letter telling what you are learning on furlough that will make you a better missionary. This is especially good if you can tell experiences in churches that helped you. That is a shot in the arm for the church and will also help other churches get ideas.

If you have taken classes that helped or stimulated you, tell something about them. Your readers are interested in many things — just as you are. And don't feel that they must be "religious" classes. Courses on history, sociology, psychology, business administration, computers, etc., will help supporters know that you want to be up-to-date and growing intellectually. And of course if you took courses in missiology, tell a bit of what has helped you.

Furlough affords missionaries the opportunity to write from a unique perspective. You may reflect on your work from a distance after several months' absence. A letter of this nature will greatly benefit you as well as your reader.

While on furlough you will undoubtedly meet new friends who want to become your prayer and support partners. Make sure you have their names and addresses. Give them two or three of your prayer letters. Write them to give background on yourself and your missionary duties, along with your best personal missionary story. Thank them for their willingness to pray. Be sure to send thank-you notes if you stayed in someone's home or enjoyed a meal, and include a prayer letter with your thank you.

You need prayer support while on furlough, as well as when you return to your adopted land. Give your new prayer partners a good start with a memorable letter.

Offer Fresh Insights

You may offer fresh insights into the religious and cultural life of your homeland. Cast your comments in positive rather than negative terms; describe your feelings and the adjustments you've made rather than attack the people or the churches you've visited.

Don't bore the reader with "housekeeping details," which contribute little to their overall understanding of missions. Don't write an inventory of everything you've done, such as what day you attended which meeting at camp or what weekend you visited which church.

Furlough letters should be warm and full of appreciation for your supporters at home. Note how one missionary built additional prayer support for herself and her adopted land. Her letter also gives the reader an "inside view" of a missionary and the purpose of furlough.

> How does it feel to be home on furlough?
>
> HOW DO I ANSWER THAT ONE? So many have asked it. So many thoughts come to me about it — BUT —
>
> How can I express my appreciation and ineffectiveness while talking to a housewife who prays and works in a kitchen paneled with missionary picture and maps? Can I explain the warmth filling me when I hear a Christian whom I have never seen before say, "I've been praying for you?" Can I measure the pleasure of knowing every letter received for five years was kept and the prayer requests remembered? Can I be thankful enough for the pure faith of a little child who kneels with the family and prays for the missionary as though she were a life-long friend?

Perhaps the answer is more than feeling and seeing; more than prayer and dedication. It is the give and take — the sharing with the people behind the lines. He may be the pastor who declares, "I would have gone, but God closed the door, so I'll stay and work for you here." She may be one of the administrative officials who plans the publicity, handles the money of the society and shares in the task of arousing sleepy Christians.

Everyone knows the gloomier side of furlough feelings too. There is the constant circle of buses, planes, cars, meetings, conferences and always one more step with a loaded suitcase. Add to that the pressure of schedules, the inadequacy of letters to keep in touch with the field, the loneliness in goodbyes and always the heart-cry to GET BACK TO CONGO!

YES, THIS IS BEING HOME ON FURLOUGH! All the praise and pain — the fruitfulness and frailty — the sacrifice and sharing — all of that YOU and ME feeling rolled into one reaction. With it all, I find myself praying, "They're behind me, Lord. They're praying me through. So help me, Lord, not to be impatient. Keep them faithful as I falter and learn of Thee. But send me back, Lord. Send me quickly. Furlough feels fine, BUT CONGO IS WAITING."

Keep Supporters Informed

Your friends and supporters are interested in you and the work on the field, even when you are away on furlough, sometimes referred to as "home assignment." If you have news about happenings in the field while you are away, share them with your supporters. Their continued prayers and support are important for the success of your work, so keep them up-to-date.

The following letter provides a meaningful bridge between home assignment and your return to the field:

Home Assignment

News from Eleanor while out of Africa No 8. Dec

A great deal has happened since my last prayer letter. So much, that I now understand better why the term "furlough" has been coined "home assignment"!

There have been several major changes for me during this time — sometimes more, it seemed, than I would ever have asked for. Some were expected; others not. But throughout them all the Lord has shown His constancy and His faithfulness.

On my way home, I had a wonderful few days in Zimbabwe, visiting dear friends and re-experiencing the environment of my teens and early adulthood. Even the sadness of the drought could not mar this relaxed and meaningful time for me.

Tracts Ready for Distribution

The tracts were finalized before I left: there are now 200,000 tracts printed and ready for distribution. Pray that the Lord will use the tracts to change people's lives.

Writer's Centre

In my last letter, I mentioned briefly a little idea I had of setting up a Writers Training Centre in Rethy. I was invited to put this dream on paper earlier this year and indeed did so. Things in Africa do not normally happen fast. But in this instance, the speed with which a vague dream became a vision and now a project is remarkable.

Thank you once again for your partnership. I thank the Lord for you.

With love in Him, Eleanor

Generate Follow-Up Prayer

The impact of a furlough letter can be far-reaching. Consider the prayers and the funds that this missionary's letter will continue to generate after she leaves for the mission field:

Dear Susan:

As I lay awake the other night for a long while in the moonlight, I pondered the problem of **what to take.**

You see, I am within three months or so of packing, final medical exams, visa application and boarding my flight. Here among my things on the table in my room is the note from the Chicago office: "We have a flight date for you. Is June 29 all right?"

The **things** I listed long ago to pack, and my family of churches are all helping in ways superabundant: a rose-colored blanket, sheets, Bible study books...The boys' and girls' club in Oak Park, has been especially hard at work.

List of Things NOT to be Taken

1. Time clock — too rigid a schedule
2. Introversion —lead in shoes which makes visitation hard, the inner shrinking when someone calls at the door
3. Fear — of the "battlefront," of the future, of the tangle of group-relationships, of the Communist shadow
4. Laziness
5. An unruly, untamed "little member" — what havoc it works — and lots more—

Benjamin and Evelyn Kent, sponsors of the club, said to me once, "We notice you never give the club's name in your letters." My problem, I told them, was to have space to explain — for the club's name is the **"Beabouts."** There are about 40 of them, with Luke 2:49 for their motto and theme — "Wist ye not that I must be about my Father's business?"

They are a lively bunch, and one of the features of each Sunday evening's meeting is a cash register around which they gather in gloriously orderly disorder to give their offerings for this missionary to Japan. I introduce them to you now, for those of you who receive these prayer letters get them via the folding, stamping and mailing efforts of this club. Since September their offerings have gone for items for me to take back to Japan. Talk about being blessed!

One of our missionaries, preparing for furlough, wrote of "things to be thrown away" and "souvenirs" and "things to be sorted." I did some

List of Things to Take
Things Imperative Regardless of Cost

1. Faith — deep-down conviction in every circumstance that my Father is in control
2. Love — with gentleness; easy to be entreated
3. Availability — always available to the people
4. Humility — to serve, not to even miss not being served
5. Abiding — based on being completely dependent upon God — and so much more.

sorting the night I lay awake — and came up with some things I want to be sure **not** to take back with me and things I must have, no matter how stiff the price. These things **you** can help me with — by prayer. Will you?

While on furlough, what should I write? And to whom should I write?

1. Have I personally thanked my prayer and funding partners? Have I given my partners reasons for continuing to pray for me now and in the future?

2. Have I shown my partners that I care for them by asking about their families and concerns?

3. Have I written follow-up letters to new partners I've gained while on furlough?

4. Have I shared accomplishments, prayer concerns, dreams and hopes with all my partners?

Postscripts

"...good prayer letters and steady prayer support are essential for the success of your mission."

Postscripts include three additional items: (i) hints for short-termers; (ii) helps for new career missionaries; (iii) a test to check the readability of your letters.

Hints for Short-termers

Today many short-term missionaries are joining career missionarics on the field.

A good letter is a good letter whether from a career missionary or a short-termer. But there are some particular problems and opportunities for short-termers.

- Make clear your status as a short-term missionary. Explain what you are doing (i.e. nurse, teacher, carpenter, accountant), and how your skills are being used. Short-termers must define their work well.
- Be sure to clarify WHY you are there as a short-term missionary and HOW you hope your contribution will enhance the work of the career missionaries. Tell about the missionaries with whom you are working. That will build prayer support for them as well as you.
- Give details about your specific project and how it relates to the total work and aims of the mission. What do you hope to accomplish? Remind your readers how long you will be on the field.
- Your letters can give the "first-sight, first-smell, first-sound" impressions of a new person in that land. Career missionaries can do that only once — when they first arrive. This kind of detail makes your mission field and your experiences come alive to the reader. It builds prayer support because readers will remember your experiences. Don't neglect your golden opportunity.

- Tell the truth. If you are lonely, say so. If you feel frustrated by lack of language skills and knowledge of the culture, say so. If you are having a hard time getting used to the different food, say so — and explain what you are eating and how it differs from your diet at home. But be sure to put the blame on yourself — not on the country or the diet! Your readers will empathize.
- Tell them how to pray for you. Be specific (i.e. "Pray that I can become a real friend to Juan in spite of our different cultures. Pray that I'll be able to adapt to his ways.").

Remember that you, a short-termer, ARE a missionary. Your supporters and prayer partners see you that way. Thus, good prayer letters and steady prayer support are essential for the success of your mission.

Helps for New Career Missionaries

Before you go, write. Don't wait until you get to the field to write your first letter to those who promised to be your supporters. After introducing your work to new supporters it would be a mistake to neglect keeping them informed. Do you want them to pray for you during the difficult support-raising period? Then keep in touch with them!

You may be wondering, what can you write about? Consider these possibilities:

- What you are doing to learn about the field to which you are going.
- Contacts you are having with nationals from that field — perhaps international students, etc.—and what you are learning from them.
- Good experiences you are having as you travel and meet churches and individuals.
- Progress reports — financial, emotional, spiritual. Let the readers see into your own heart and what is happening there. Of course, there are personal things you cannot tell, but there are many others that you can share.

Here is an excellent example of a letter sent to supporters before leaving for the field:

David & Nadia Johansen

Missionaries to Niger

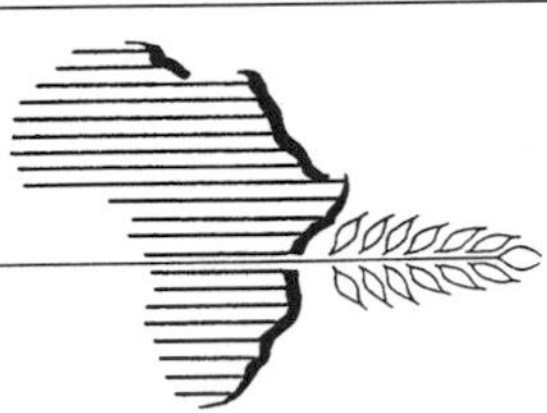

Dear Pastor and Friends of the Work in West Africa,

WE HAVE JUST MET OUR REDUCED BUDGET! This itineration has taken us to churches across eleven states over a year and five months. Being able to tell of the pioneer work in Niger to your Sunday school classes, youth, WM's, cell groups and regular services has caused our heart to rejoice concerning your vision. Yet, we are eager to return to the land where God has called us to labor. Remember to send in your pledge form to Springfield (account #2261287). Additional funds can always be put to use, so please pray and respond accordingly.

OUR TICKETS ARE PURCHASED. Despite the difficulty in booking a flight on short notice during heavy holiday travel, some seats opened up and we will be leaving on December 26, 1994, for Africa. P-t-L! Our first stop will be at our parents in Dakar, Senegal. Nadia hasn't been home since 1986 and it'll be my first visit.

WE GO REJOICING TO BRING IN THE SHEAVES: To God be the glory for what He has done through you by enabling us to continue the harvesting in Niger. This ministry is the fruit of the entire body of Christ working together. **THANK-YOU** for becoming partners, faithfully praying and giving to further the gospel in the unreached areas of West Africa. "The people walking in darkness have seen a great light...", Isaiah 9:2 (NIV).

PRAYER REQUESTS:

1) Presidential elections on Dec. 31, 1994.
2) Stability & peace in Niger
3) Our visit to Nadia's parents Muslim home
4) Rada, Nadia's sister
5) Journey mercies

PRAISE REPORTS:

1) Financial clearance
2) Airline tickets
3) Supporting churches

May God's grace and peace abound in your midst! Let us jointly celebrate and declare the purpose of Jesus' birth till the whole world knows.

In the Lord of the Harvest,
with immense gratitude,

The Johansens

Ten Commandments of Good Writing

1. Keep words, sentences and paragraphs short. Sentences should vary in structure and length.
2. Prefer the simple to the complex.
3. Use familiar words.
4. Avoid unnecessary words — cut ruthlessly as if you were an editor.
5. Use active not passive verbs.
6. Write the way you talk.
7. Tie your letters to your reader's experience. Proceed from the known to the unknown.
8. Use concrete words your reader can visualize. Abstract words dull your writing.
9. Add variety. Develop your own personal style.
10. Write to express — not to impress.

Fog Index

One popular formula for measuring the readability of your writing is that of Robert Gunning, commonly known as the Fog Index.

1. Count sample of 100 words.
2. Count number of difficult words (three or more syllables).
3. Compute average number of words per sentence.
4. Add answer for (2) to the answer for (3). Multiply the sum by the constant 0.4. Your answer is an approximate grade-in-school reading level.

Readers Digest has a Fog Index of 8; *Time*, 10, even the *Atlantic Monthly*, commonly considered a highbrow magazine, has a Fog Index of 12 (high-school senior level). If you really want to communicate with your home constituency, probably your prayer letter should not have a Fog Index rating of more than 10.

The Ease of E-mail

Today all but a few corners of the world have access to e-mail, so more overseas workers are using it and finding it an easy way to keep in touch with family and friends. You'll still want to send a hard copy of your letter to those who haven't requested e-mail, but the new technology can save you time and money and make it easier for many of your supporters to stay in touch with you.

The advantages are obvious. You save postage and printing costs. You can send it right from the field, rather than asking someone back home to do it, as many workers do. You can personalize some of the letters and/or segment your list into groups such as family, close friends, churches, or any other special groups. E-mail is also easy for the receiver to forward to someone else. Some churches, for example, regularly forward copies of e-mail letters to members of their missions committee, and especially interesting letters are often "passed around" by e-mail.

The disadvantages are few but important. Not everyone has access to e-mail, especially not at home. Many older folks, who may be some of your best prayer supporters, do not use e-mail. And many people, even though they have access to e-mail, still prefer to get a hard copy in the mail.

Ask folks to send you their e-mail address if they'd prefer to get your letter that way. Keep putting your e-mail address as a P.S. on the bottom of your hard-copy letters, and after awhile you'll find your e-mail list growing, and your hard-copy list diminishing.

Workers in countries where the government is not friendly to Christian missions have to be careful, of course. If you want folks to reply to you by e-mail, you'll need to warn them not to use certain words or expressions or to write about certain topics. Your mission directors will give you guidance on that.

The writing in some e-mail letters today tends to be brief and choppy, and this raises the question of writing style. Should the style of writing in e-mail differ from that in hard copy?

Good writing is good writing, whether it comes by snail mail or by e-mail. Avoid slang-ridden, breezy or choppy writing, just because the medium is different. Good, acceptable English prose will always do a better job of communicating.

E-mail does, however, demand a few considerations. For one thing you'll want to keep your letters short, not much more than

500 words or so. If the letter is too long, readers will tend to scroll through it quickly. It's also doubly important to get a fast start in e-mail with something that draws readers in quickly. Your readers may be dear, close friends, but if you ramble and don't give them a good reason to read on, they have only to make one click of the mouse and your letter goes to the recycle bin.

Beware of attachments, however, that require certain software to open. Some recipients won't have the necessary technical expertise or software to do that.

Personal websites are growing more and more popular and can be a wonderful way to let people know what God is doing in your life and ministry. These can be a great help in recruiting short-term workers.

Be sure to put an e-mail response device on your site for people who want more information. You can put photos, art, articles, maps, and links to other sites on your site. However, don't depend on a web site to keep people informed. Only a small percentage of your supporters will take the time to browse your web site to keep up with you. You have to go to them first. In your e-mail, include the link to your website so that readers simply have to click on that link to visit the site. — Ron Wilson, MAI

Add Life to Your Ministry Letters

Orchestra conductors often say something like this to their musicians: "Let's play that passage again, and this time, let's do it with *feeling*. Make it come alive. Compel the audience to listen."

We could say the same thing about the letters of many folks in ministry. Their prose is correct, the form is right, even the topic has great potential interest. But something's missing. The writing lacks life. The letters are impersonal, remote. They could have been written by a corporation. We can easily put them down and go on to something more interesting, more compelling.

What does it take to write a letter that someone just can't put down? The qualities of writing I describe here will add life to your ministry letters and gain faithful readers who will look forward to the next one.

Raise a picture in the mind

The best writing helps the reader to see. It raises pictures in the mind. It puts the reader right there in the scene and helps him or her to touch, hear, see or smell. These concrete examples stick in readers' minds.

Here's an example from a letter from the Philippines:

"Minda lived on Smokey Mountain, a growing heap of garbage at the edge of the city. She was one of a community of some 18,000 squatters living on the fetid mound and earning their livelihood from the abandoned, rusting and rotting refuse. At night or when it rained she lived under a piece of once-yellow plastic, moving it every week as her neighbors drove her out. Sewerage ran in front of her makeshift tent, and the ground under her was mushy."

A picture like this not only sticks in the mind and tempts the reader to learn more, it may also carry a truth we want to get across. Let's say you want to convey the simple, biblical idea that God's love is unconditional. That's what Jesus did when he told the story of the prodigal son. The very mention of it brings to my mind a white-bearded and stooped old man, running down the road toward his ragged, foul-smelling son who has returned in disgrace. Both have tears in their eyes. The son bows his head in shame. The old man kisses the son. This is my picture, of course, and the one in your mind may not be the same. That's okay. The important thing is that you have a picture and this picture stays in your mind and conveys the idea that God's love comes without any conditions attached.

Write the Way You Talk

Why is it that when some people start to write, they make it such hard work? They seem to put on a "writer's hat." They groan and agonize, trying to find big words or clever ways of saying things. Just start to talk and put the words down. Be direct. Say it simply and sit down. It's okay to use contractions. Sentences may be short.

Test your prose by reading it aloud. It should fall easily over the tongue and read well. If you stumble over it, so will the reader.

Pull off Your Mask

If you were sitting down over coffee or tea in the home of a close friend, you'd reveal your feelings. You'd let your friend see a little of what's going on underneath, the real you. If you're ecstatic about what God is doing, your friend will know it. If you're discouraged or struggling with relationships, you'd talk about it, ask for prayer.

As you know, there is a misconception abroad that Christian workers are a spiritual step above the rest of the church. They don't get depressed, lonely, make big mistakes, get a little lazy at times, worry, yell at their children or have trouble admitting mistakes.

The quickest way to dispel this myth is to reveal these struggles to the readers — people who struggle with the same things. Rather than scoff at you or wonder what's wrong with you, they will find their hearts going out to you. You'll become real to them in a new way. In other words, they'll identify with you. Your vulnerability will make you become real.

I don't mean you have to bare your soul in every letter. I'm not talking about putting your darkest thoughts on paper. Just let your readers know that you have problems, too. Be transparent!

You may never hear about it, but I believe that as your readers draw closer to you in your deep joys and struggles, and see that you are just as they are — a struggling sinner — the prayers of the saints for you will rise in great numbers toward heaven.

Here's one more example that does all that I've talked about here. It puts the reader right in the picture. It sounds the way this writer talks, and it reveals something going on deep in her heart. Here's how she began her letter:

"Dear Friends: Yen's rooster woke me up. Yen's children threw trash in my yard. Yen stood at my window while I had company and asked what we were eating. Yen spit. Yen's chickens dirtied my doorstep. Yen was my next door neighbor and I wasn't too impressed with her. She was a thorn in my flesh."

Don't you want to read more? That's what I mean by *compelling* — a letter your readers can't put down.

—By Ron Wilson, MAI

10 More Points for Prayer Letters

1. Put Foreign News in a Familiar Context

Put foreign news and statistics in a frame of reference your readers will recognize. For example:

"In 1984, with 14 million people, greater Sao Paulo had more people than Honduras, Nicaragua, El Salvador, and Costa Rica combined."

"Every day more than 150 million children under 5 in developing countries go to bed hungry. That's more than the entire population of Brazil."

"A survey revealed that only 3 in every 1,000 people in Caracas are evangelical Christians. That's like my home town having only one church with 12 members."

2. Use Maps

Show people where you are working. Many readers haven't the slightest idea where Kenya or Thailand or Honduras are located.

3. Establish Points of Contact

If we help our readers see that what happens in one foreign country will affect them—and vice versa—then our news and experience will take on new meaning.

For example, in an article on Latin America's drug trade, *The Miami Herald* quoted one government official:

"If we wanted tomatoes, they (Latin Americans) would grow tomatoes. If we wanted cantaloupes, they would grow cantaloupes. It's just too bad that what we want is dope."

4. Use Foreign Words Sparingly

Don't try to impress your reader with your language ability. This often turns off readers. Use foreign words only if there is a good reason for doing so.

5. Avoid Acronyms

Just as you avoid foreign words, stay away from the alphabet soup, such as CLAI, CONELA, UNILIT, CLAME, etc. The average reader won't have a clue what they stand for.

6. **Show, Don't Tell**

   Help your readers *see* the place and the people where you work. But don't get carried away with adjectives.

7. **Avoid "Content Idolatry"**

   You learned about the culture by long hard work, but don't take it out on your readers by telling them everything you've learned. Don't give them more than they can handle. There should be a good reason for the content, not just for the sake of their education.

8. **Eliminate Spiritual Clichés and Mission Lingo**

   Find substitutes for worn-out phrases such as: believers, accept Christ, fellowship, won to Christ, share, foreign field, mission field, contextualization, church planting.

9. **Use a Little Humor**

   A little humor will help shatter the stereotype of missionaries as perpetually serious, if not dour. Prove wrong the editor who wrote, "Missionaries love to be preachy, angry, folksy or whiny."

10. **Write on Things You Feel Passionately About**

    People are attracted to the human element in a prayer letter, as well as to things they can apply to their own lives. If you feel "blah" about a subject, they will, too.

—By John Maust, MAI

Prayer Letter Phobia

As a missionary I discovered the significance of regular, monthly and occasionally extraordinary letters to my supporters. This was impressed on me by the constant feedback I received as a prayer letter writer.

I soon learned that some mission committees read those letters at their monthly meetings and that some churches published excerpts from those letters for the whole congregation once a month.

Committees and churches heard regularly from me, and they reported their appreciation in letters back to me. On furlough I was once introduced as the missionary "who believed in the importance of the church at home" because I wrote so often.

I concluded that keeping a vibrant connection with my sending team was just as vital as commitment to my field of service or the people to whom I ministered. As a result, I never lost a supporting church or individual. Later, as pastor of a church helping to support some 50 missionaries, I was further persuaded of the significance of writing those regular letters.

Some missionaries wrote rarely. "Too busy," or "We didn't have anything to write" were responses I recognized as subtle insults.

"Too busy" suggested the home team was unimportant or unnecessary to the missionary. "Nothing to write" implied a business rather than a love relationship.

"One of the busiest and, I must add, most successful, missionaries I have ever known wrote me a personal letter in longhand every month for many years. I came to love that man. I couldn't help it. The information was usually personal, his interest always affirming. And his expressed intent was gratitude for "our partnership in the Gospel."

When this missionary reached retirement, I invited him to join our church staff. I concluded that anyone who wrote prayer letters so enthusiastically and faithfully had to be an exceptional missionary. He was and still is. And so is everyone who writes such letters as ministry.

As the Apostle Paul demonstrated in the First Century, letters are a vital part of the missionary calling.

—By Art Brown, Westmont, IL,
a former missionary in Europe and retired pastor of 22 years from Western Springs (IL) Baptist Church

MEDIA ASSOCIATES INTERNATIONAL, INC.
"Discovering Talent: Equipping for Service"

Media Associates International, Inc. (MAI) serves the worldwide Christian church by training and encouraging Christian media personnel to become skilled communicators of the Gospel especially through the printed page. MAI provides on-site strategic guidance and technical assistance to national Christian leaders and missionaries involved in print ministries in Africa, Asia, Latin America and the Middle East, as well as Central and East Europe.

MAI is a not-for-profit 501(c)(3) publicly supported Christian agency. It is a member of International Foreign Mission Association (IFMA) and also the Evangelical Council for Financial Accountability (ECFA). In 1987 MAI absorbed Evangelical Literature Overseas (ELO) through a merger.

MAI is also a registered British Charity (No. 328568) with an office in England. It is a member of Global Connections in the U.K.

Media Associates International, Inc.
P.O. Box 218, Bloomingdale, IL 60108-0218 USA
TEL: 630-893-1977, FAX: 630-893-1141
MaiLITTWORLD@cs.com
www.littworld.org

Media Associates International
Concorde House, Grenville Place, Mill Hill,
London NW7 3SA England
TEL: (020) 8906 9768, FAX: (020) 8959 3678

Other Resources from MAI

Besides ***How To Write Missionary Letters***, MAI has the following helpful resources:

Books:

- ***An Asian Palette***, Armour Publishing (1998, 122pp, paperback). Having experienced God's touch on their lives twelve Asian men and women write about their writing craft. Wherever you may be in your personal journey as a writer, there is something in this book for you.

- ***An Unfading Vision*** by Edward England (1998, 184pp, paperback) is an invaluable resource for anyone involved in equipping and encouraging Christian publishers, editors and writers. But even if you are not engaged in publishing, you'll find it a fascinating read. You will sense afresh the power of words in an information-saturated world.

- ***Journeys Into Creativity***, Africa Christian Press (1994, 160pp, paperback). Eleven African Christian authors give personal insights into the joys, struggles and hopes of writing books, novels, plays and columns pertinent to African readers. Read what motivates them to keep writing.

- ***Servant of Words: A Tribute to James L. Johnson, Mentor to Writers and Communicators*** (Moody Press, 1992, 220pp, quality paperback). Moving personal accounts about author and novelist, Jim Johnson, and his extraordinary impact on lives. Jim Johnson directed Evangelical Literature Overseas (ELO) for many years and was a founding director of MAI.

More Resources from MAI on next page

Newsletters:

- ***Profile***
  This quarterly newsletter gives you the latest reports on MAI's print media training activities around the world.

- ***Trainer Network***
  Practical tools and tips for print media trainers are found in every issue of this quarterly newsletter available for an $8.00 annual subscription.

Additional titles and current price quotes can be found on MAI's web site, www.littworld.org or by contact with the MAI office.

Media Associates International
P.O. Box 218
Bloomingdale, IL 60108-0218, USA
Tel: Int'l code + 630-893-1977, Fax: Int'l code + 630-893-1141
MaiLITTWORLD@cs.com